MIGHTY MACHINES

Police Cars

by Kay Manolis

BELLWETHER MEDIA • MINNEAPOLIS, MN

Note to Librarians, Teachers, and Parents:

Blastoff! Readers are carefully developed by literacy experts and combine standards-based content with developmentally appropriate text.

Level 1 provides the most support through repetition of high-frequency words, light text, predictable sentence patterns, and strong visual support.

Level 2 offers early readers a bit more challenge through varied simple sentences, increased text load, and less repetition of high-frequency words.

Level 3 advances early-fluent readers toward fluency through increased text and concept load, less reliance on visuals, longer sentences, and more literary language.

Level 4 builds reading stamina by providing more text per page, increased use of punctuation, greater variation in sentence patterns, and increasingly challenging vocabulary.

Level 5 encourages children to move from "learning to read" to "reading to learn" by providing even more text, varied writing styles, and less familiar topics.

Whichever book is right for your reader, Blastoff! Readers are the perfect books to build confidence and encourage a love of reading that will last a lifetime!

This edition first published in 2008 by Bellwether Media.

No part of this publication may be reproduced in whole or in part without written permission of the publisher. For information regarding permission, write to Bellwether Media Inc., Attention: Permissions Department, Post Office Box 19349, Minneapolis, MN 55419.

Library of Congress Cataloging-in-Publication Data
Manolis, Kay.
  Police cars / by Kay Manolis.
    p. cm. — (Blastoff! readers. Mighty machines)
  Includes bibliographical references and index.
Summary: "Simple text and full color photographs introduce young readers to police cars. Intended for students in kindergarten through third grade"—Provided by publisher.
  ISBN-13: 978-1-60014-179-9 (hardcover : alk. paper)
  ISBN-10: 1-60014-179-X (hardcover : alk. paper)
  1. Police vehicles—Juvenile literature. I. Title.

HV7936.V4M36 2008
629.222—dc22   2007040423

Contents

Police cars
are used by
police officers.

Police officers
help people in
emergencies.

Police cars
patrol
the streets.

SCOUT

CA EXEMPT
1204682

Police cars have flashing lights and a **siren**. These tell drivers that police cars are coming.

Police cars have **two-way radios**. This officer can talk with officers in other places.

two-way radio

Police cars have **radar**. Officers use radar to check how fast cars are moving.

Police officers turn on the siren and flashing lights. They stop a car that is moving too fast.

Officers write a **ticket** for the driver.

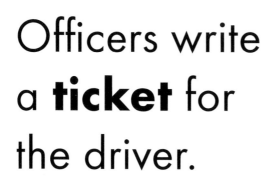

Police cars can also lead parades. Police cars help officers do good work.

Glossary

emergencies—serious problems or times of danger

patrol—to move around an area checking to make sure people are safe

radar—a tool that shows how fast cars are moving

siren—a horn that makes a loud sound; police cars use sirens to warn cars that they are coming.

ticket—a warning or punishment given to someone who breaks a driving law

two-way radios—radios used to talk with people in other places

To Learn More

AT THE LIBRARY

Auerbach, Annie. *Police on Patrol*. New York: Little Simon, 2003.

McGuire, Leslie. *Big Mike's Police Car*. New York: Random House, 2003.

Roberts, Cynthia. *Police Cars*. Mankato, Minn.: The Child's World, 2007.

ON THE WEB

Learning more about mighty machines is as easy as 1, 2, 3.

1. Go to www.factsurfer.com

2. Enter "mighty machines" into search box.

3. Click the "Surf" button and you will see a list of related web sites.

With factsurfer.com, finding more information is just a click away.

Index

The images in this book are reproduced through the courtesy of: Brad Sauter, front cover; Shaun Lowe, p. 5; Benn Mitchell/Getty Images, p. 7; Kanwarjit Singh Boparai, p. 9; Dennis MacDonald/Age fotostock, p. 11; David R. Frazier Photolibrary, Inc/Alamy, p. 13; Brad Sauter, p. 15; Jeff Smith/Alamy, p. 17; Frances Twitty, p. 19; Kanwarjit Singh Boparai, p. 21.